just being honest

just being honest

reflections on trying to be christian

Dave Magill

Gilead Books Publishing
www.GileadBooks.com

First published in Great Britain, May 2008
by Gilead Books Publishing
Corner Farm
West Knapton
Malton
North Yorkshire YO17 8JB
www.GileadBooks.com

British Library Cataloguing-in-Publication Data
A catalogue record for this book is available
From the British Library

ISBN-13: 978-0-9558099-1-0

Thank you

To Joanne
To our families
To Dave, Josh, Pete and the JPs
To everyone who is in my story and has affected my life.
To Jesus.

Introduction

I don't really know what you are meant to write in an introduction. I never read them when I read a book. I always skip it. My mind tells me that if it wasn't good enough to make it into a chapter, then I shouldn't waste my time reading it. Yet here I am trying to write an introduction to what appears to be a book written by me.

I never thought I had a book in me. I have never had much difficulty writing songs or poems, they have always been easy. They are short and don't necessarily have to mean anything or be structured in any logical way. A book feels a little different, a little more challenging. People who write books are always people who are much more intelligent than me and use words that I don't understand. My sister Julie, she is an author. She has enough words in her head to fill a library. She has big ideas and understands the writings of people like Rutherford and John Calvin. I don't even like to hold books by Rutherford and John Calvin. They hurt my head.

So it comes as a bit of a shock to me that I am writing a book. I'll tell you how it happened. I was sitting at the computer in our spare room and thought I would try and write a song, but not in the normal way I write a song where the inspiration comes to me. This time I would try and develop a strategy to write a song. In a way I tried to force a song. My first thought was to pick a topic. I opened a Word document (other word processing packages are available) and typed the word God. I then began to write some ideas about God. Two hours later I had typed 2000 words. I was amazed. Where had it all come from and how come it made sense? Some of those words became the chapter in this book named God.

The next day I sat down again and typed about the bible. Again I wrote more than I thought I could. Now I have written a whole bunch of words and told a whole lot of stories and I guess I have written a book.

So who is it for? What's it about? Well I guess it is for anyone, but I reckon people who are between 16 and 25 will appreciate it the most, just a feeling I have. What's it about? Well, a lot of things really. I guess it is just some thoughts on the things that I think are important in my life as a follower of Jesus. There is no real order to the things in here. There is no hypothesis and no conclusion, no beginning, middle or end. It just is what it is: a book that has a bunch of ideas about a bunch of different ideas.

In a sense I am trying to be honest about what I believe to be true about certain things. I don't think there is anything very groundbreaking in here and I don't think that I am teaching anyone anything new. I hope that all of it is the Truth, but that is not what I set out to write about. I just wanted to be honest.

The bible

I'm not very good at the bible. Not in the western evangelical sense of being good at the bible. Let me explain. It is my understanding that to be a "good Christian" these days you have to know word for word a vast chunk of the bible. You have to know the structure of Romans and the linguistic genius of Genesis. Good Christians have whole conversations about passages of the bible without even mentioning the content. Today I walked through York with Big Al. We talked for five minutes about Revelation 5. He talked about the intricacy of it, the excitement of "the search" and "all that happened before verse 4". I smiled and nodded. I said things like, "uh-huh" and "yeah" but I had no idea what Revelation 5 was about. This wasn't the first time this has happened.

I have listened to debates between "good Christians" in which no one ever quotes a word of scripture. Instead their arguments are a list of references. I feel incredibly uncomfortable in these situations. I have a theology degree, I should really know what the bible says and where it says it, but the truth is I don't. I live in fear that one day I will be exposed as a "bad Christian", that I will be branded with a symbol that tells everyone I don't know my bible. I feel embarrassed sometimes that I read the New Living Translation. I claim I use it because of its good translation policy, ie it translates thoughts rather than word for word. In reality, I find it easier to understand. Other people use the New King James Version and, if you are incredibly holy, the "original" King James Version. I do wonder how many other people like me there are who are nervous about being shown up as biblically illiterate.

I also wonder how important it is to know the bible word for word? How important is it to know chapter and verse? Even if I can remember Romans 8 off by heart, the next guy might read a different version of the bible from me and his Romans 8 will be different from mine. Is it enough to know what the bible says? Is it enough to know that all things will work together for my good if I love God? Do I need to add on Romans 8:28 for it to count as true? Do I need to remember that Jesus came to give me life to the full, or is it more important to remember that I can find it written in John 10:10? I don't know the answer. I know a lot of what the bible says, but I'm not very good at telling you where it says it. Maybe I'm making excuses for myself. I'm sure it is important to know the references, but perhaps not as much as we think. I have sat in Sunday school classes and observed 7 year olds recite huge chunks of scripture word perfectly, only to be denied their sticker because they said Romans 9 instead of 8. It is quite a strange phenomenon. I guess I am just reacting to it.

I have another problem with the bible. Well, my problem isn't really with the bible; it is more to do with the way we treat it. I'll give an example. Imagine that you are in a church. The pastor stands up and says the sermon is going to be about the story of the feeding of the five thousand. Everybody in the room thinks, oh yeah, five loaves, two fish, 12 baskets of leftovers. Nobody reacts. What has happened to us? FIVE THOUSAND PEOPLE!!! FIVE LOAVES TWO FISH!!! LEFTOVERS!!! That story is amazing. We should be scratching our heads in wonder at what Jesus did. What did it look like when he broke a bit off? Did the bread get smaller as he broke it? Did people notice what was happening?

The whole way through the Gospels and in Acts groups of people are described as being astonished by what God does. These days when we read these stories we just about smile. How have we allowed ourselves to become so familiar with these stories that we don't even notice the wonder in them? I am fighting to win back my wonder. I want to read the bible and be shocked like the first time I heard these stories. I want to be shocked that God chose David as king. I want to be shocked that the walls fell down at Jericho. I want to feel sick at the unfair trial of Jesus. I want to cry when Stephen is martyred. I want the bible to be real again. I want to allow it to be living and active.

Joanne and I had our friends Rachel and Michael over for Sunday lunch this weekend. They have two small sons, Joshua and Peter. Peter has just had his first birthday and is very curious. He puts everything in his mouth and picks up just about anything he can lift. He looks at things and studies things. Joshua, who is three, asks questions. Why, daddy? How, mummy? Small things become interesting; nothing becomes everything when you are a child. That is the kind of curiosity and wonder I want to experience when I read the bible.

This is why we need preachers. Mike Yaconelli said preachers exist to bring the stories back to life. I love nothing more than listening to a good preacher who can ignite my imagination and involve me in the stories of the bible. Problem is, it isn't the most popular kind of preaching. People will choose to hear intellectual argument and critical thought over storytelling. It's amazing how many times I have heard sermons on parables of Jesus that end up being discussions of the literary constructs and linguistic patterns of Jesus' words.

I learnt in bible college that to understand the bible there are certain rules to apply: context, content, repeated phrases and so on. I'm not so sure though. Those are the same tools that I learnt when I studied Macbeth at school, and I am sure of one thing: the bible was never meant to read like Shakespeare. Jesus could have chosen intellectual arguments but he didn't. Instead he told stories. Jesus could have held complicated moral discourse with the Pharisees. Instead he talked about soil, rain and the sun with peasants. Jesus could have concocted formulae and philosophical theory, but he chose to tell stories. Nowadays we put that down to his audience being uneducated – shepherds and fishermen who couldn't understand the intricacies of theology. How arrogant! What if Jesus had never meant his gospel to be intellectually complicated, no matter how much we want it to be?

It is much easier to feel validated in front of your critics if your belief system is complex. It feels much better if you can argue your point with your colleagues. But the fact is that what we believe is foolishness to those who don't believe it. No matter how impressive your argument is. I am beginning to understand why Jesus told us that we had to be like children to enter the Kingdom of God. It's because children can handle the simple; adults can't. We have to complicate things.

I am so thankful to God that he has allowed me to do what I do. I get to hang out with some of the most exciting Christians in the world. I have spent the last two weeks with teenagers. I have learnt more about what the bible means from these guys than I ever have from sermons. An example? I have heard about 20 sermons on the Great Commission. Each one sounds the same: it discusses the meaning of the verse. What did Jesus mean by "go"? What did Jesus mean by "the world"? We discuss whether when Jesus said "preach" he meant literally with words, or was Saint Francis right when he told us to try and do it without words? By the end of these kinds of sermons the last thing I want to do is tell anyone about Jesus. All I need is a rest.

The teenagers I know read that verse and came up with the idea of going into the park to tell people about God. No questions! Jesus said go to the world. The world includes the park, right? So let's go. We spent a sunny Tuesday afternoon chatting to random people about God in the park.

What happened to me as I got older? How did I go from being like these teenagers to being an intellectual reader of the bible? I am praying these days that I will become more like these young people. I want to read my bible like they do. I want to ask who wrote Psalms out of interest like they do, not because I want to compare writing styles. I have so much to learn, I am glad God has surrounded me with young teachers.

I am a bible abuser. I have been given this amazing leather-bound gift from God but I abuse it. I'll explain with an example. I am a Christian so I don't do horoscopes. I laugh at the people who do. Horoscopes are ridiculous. How can one paragraph be true for the 500 million people for whom it is written? It can't. There aren't enough tall, dark, handsome men to go round all the Sagittarius women in the world. Thing is though, I treat my quiet time very much like a horoscope. What magical thing will God tell me today? But that's not what the bible is for. Yes on occasion, perhaps even regularly, my reading of scripture has miraculously been spot on for what I am facing at the specific time I read it, but most of the time it isn't. I have slipped into the idea that my quiet times are good when I am getting a direct hit for my situation. I am a bible abuser. I only like it when it suits me.

I don't think God ever intended me to read the bible that way. The bible was never meant to be a lucky charm or life guide. The bible was meant to be God's way of telling me he loves me. I am meant to read the bible and get to know him better. The direction will come, the guidance for decisions will come, but I need to break through my self-centred reading habits. I need to be more concerned about getting to know God through what he has said to me than I am about what the bible can do for me. I hate the habit I have. It is destroying my most important relationship. Pray for me that God will wake me up to the truth. He has written a letter to me because he loves me. He tells me on every page that he loves me and I read it looking for my next intellectual fix.

God

I have always believed in God. I can't remember a time that I ever thought he wasn't there. My parents brought me up that way. I sometimes try to imagine what it would be like to have discovered God if I had not been brought up in a house where he was an accepted reality. I wonder what it would have been like going home having met God that day? What my parents and siblings would have thought as I explained the experiences I had had and the things I had heard? In my version of events they all become Christians instantly as I share the story with them.

That wasn't the way it was though. I am probably quite fortunate. God has always been a part of my life whether indirectly through the lives of my family or directly through my own relationship with him. My second earliest memory is a prayer. I remember talking to God in my bed as a very young child. My earliest memory is driving my pedal car into a wall aged three but I would hardly call that a spiritual experience.

There are times that my mind wanders and I begin to think what the consequences would be if I was wrong. I read an article once for my one module in sociology that suggests humans are socially conditioned to believe in a benevolent creator. Sometimes I wonder what my life would be like if that was true? Would it change at all? Generally though I am very sure he is up there, watching us as they say. I'm not alone in this; many people have had a similar experience. All over the world there are people who have always had an awareness that God is there. Some like me were told he was there, others just seemed to realise it for themselves.

For me the difficulty has never been in believing that God was there. For me it has always been in knowing what he is like. Growing up in Northern Ireland I am not sure I got the chance to get to know God as a child. Instead I got to know about what he did, how he wanted me to behave and even at times how he wanted me to dress. That is what Sunday school was all about. There are photos of me aged about six wearing my "this-will-make-God-happy" suit, a mass of red curls on my head and a forced toothy grin. There I am standing in the garden with a green and white striped shirt and grey three-piece on, looking like a well-dressed dandelion posing for Granda Bob's expensive camera. I remember those days so clearly. I remember thinking God would be pleased with me if I wore my suit and got my tie straight. I don't wear suits very often anymore, but in some ways that idea has never left me. I still judge other people's closeness to God by the clothes they wear on a Sunday.

Ridiculous isn't it? Dave looks at the jeans and t-shirt but God looks at the heart.

I have other ideas of God's character ingrained in me. I only recently began to deal with the thought that God takes pleasure in sending people to hell. I never consciously concluded that it was true but deep in my thoughts it was there. I know where I got it from. Every Saturday I would listen to old guys in suits with grey hairy ears and thick-rimmed glasses taking pleasure in telling passers-by they were going to hell. I rarely remember hearing about Jesus from those guys. I'm sure somewhere along the line my mind attributed their attitude to God. Maybe it was the grey hair. I have always thought God has grey hair.

My friend Dave – I call him Average Dave because he's slightly better than me – sorted this for me recently without knowing it. We were chatting to an older couple in the Museum Gardens in York, and Dave said something like this. "We tend to think of it all wrong. God doesn't send anyone to hell. Everyone is heading there anyway. God gives us a way out of it."

You can tell that I don't have high standards. That is basic theology, a level one belief of the Christian faith. It took me 22 years of being a Christian to get it into my head. But that's why Dave is average and I am, well, below average.

That experience with the older couple worried me. I have begun to question how much of what I know of God is constructed from my experience of those who claim to know God. And I am only 27 – what about people in their 50s and 60s? Do they have these wrong ideas? And what am I passing on to the youth? Do they see my impatience and inconsistency and attribute that to God because I represent him as their youth worker?

I have begun to wonder whether or not any of us know God even one per cent as much as we think we do? I wonder how many of us know a God who is a confused blend of our fathers, teachers, pastors, friends and those guys off Christian television? How many of us pray to a God who is absent like so many fathers, or who is judgemental like so many pastors? How many of us are singing to a God who humiliates us in front of our classmates or gossips to the rest of our friends? How many of us follow a God who manipulates us out of our money to buy jets and mansions and golden pulpits to preach from? The answer is too many.

The number of people who think that God has rejected them because of a mistake they made years ago is incredible. If you talk to these people, at some point an elder or pastor or friend will have done the same thing. Or how many people feel that God is punishing them for not loving him enough? Somewhere in their history someone will have done just that. Those who claim the name of Jesus have a lot to answer for. We have slandered him more than we can begin to realise. I worry that there are young people or past acquaintances out there who know a God who looks and acts like me. How many teenagers have I snapped at? How many friends have I disappointed? Too many! How can I expect any of the people God has brought into my life to trust him, when I who represent him am so untrustworthy?

I need a change. No, I need a renewal. I need him who makes all things new to fix me. I need to lose all this baggage and then I need to find him. I need to find out who he actually is and how he feels about me. I need to know what he would do when faced with the things I face. I need to know why he loves me and whether or not he likes me. I need to know that he is patient and faithful. I need to know that when I slap him in the face with my torrent of sinfulness he will still look me in the eye and tell me he loves me. I need this more than I can even admit to myself.

So who is he? What is he like? I'll get a new page and a sharp pencil and portrait the Creator. Where do I start? What is my inspiration? Love. My mind went to love. "God is love." (1 John 4) God is not just love like the feeble attempt at love I show other people. God is unconditional, unending, unrelenting, pursuing love. Dangerous love. God is perfect, saturating, undeserved love. God is love. I have never seen this kind of love, although recently I think I came close. My friend Josh showed me a human version of it. We were on camp together. Josh went out of his way at every opportunity to serve me, to feed me, to praise me – to love me, basically. Every time I walked into a room there Josh was, placing food and a glass of cola in my hand. There was no reason for it. He got nothing back. He earned nothing from it. He just did it because he loves me. God has given Josh a gift. Josh can love people; he's good at it. Josh has shown me a little bit about God, God loves me. God gives me more than I could begin to list and for no reason other than his love for me. Breath, Joanne, food, milk, toothpaste, light, time... endless gifts of his love. God is LOVE.

God's love is an active love. Brian, Josh's dad, preached a series of sermons on God. I can remember the first thing he said: God is compassionate (Joel 2:13). God will go out of his way to change our lives with his love. His love is a compassionate love. There is a beautiful line in Exodus that shows me something of God's compassion. The writer describes how God heard the groaning of the Hebrew slaves and was concerned about them. He then breaks the laws of physics to save them. God heard the groans of a people who had lost the will to live.

God heard the cries of the slaves in Egypt and he could not ignore them.

I was at a friend's party recently and many of the guests had their children with them. The children played in the garden while the parents drank wine and ate nachos in the house. At some point during the evening a cry came from the garden. Everyone's eyes looked to the patio doors to see who was hurt, except for one mother. Before I could focus my eyes on the garden, she was out there cradling her two-year-old son in her arms, kissing and stroking his grazed knee to comfort him. That mother knew the cry of her child. She didn't have to think whether or not it was her son. Her love for that boy had propelled her into the garden. She had compassion for her son's cry. She had a love that could not sit still. That mother taught me about my Father's love, my Father's compassion. He cannot hear my cry and sit still. When I groan in the slavery I have chosen, the slavery of sin, he cannot leave me there. His love propels him to save me, because I am his child and he treasures me.

I had a dream recently. I was meant to be preparing a sermon but I made the mistake of preparing whilst lying on my bed. I fell asleep. It's not the first time this has happened. I dreamt about my sermon, I dreamt about giving it. As I woke up I was concluding my sermon, but not in the way I had planned, I had added a drama. It went something like this. I play Jesus. Adam my sidekick plays himself. He represents humanity. I look him in the eye and say I love him. He likes me too. I tell a story of how Adam told a lie. There is a pause and then Adam hits me in the face with all his might. I look back at Adam, "I love you Adam, I forgive you."

"I like you too."

Adam swears, gets drunk, judges, gossips, lusts etc. Each time he sins, he hits me with all his might. Each time I look back and tell him I love him. He likes me too. Eventually Adam realises what it means, I, Jesus, love him. I forgive him. He throws his arms around me and weeps.

"I love you too, Jesus I love you too."

That drama which we performed that night has haunted me. Not because of the beating I took, but because of the beating I have given Jesus. Over my 22 years of trying to follow him I have hit him pretty hard. What haunts me is the look of love in his eyes as he says, "I forgive you Dave". I long to be able to reply with some meaning. I do love him but my life doesn't mean it. But he knows me. He knows my heart. He knows my longing to want to love him with the love he deserves. One day maybe I will.

I am beginning to meet God. He is answering my prayers. He is allowing me to meet people and read his word, and each day I am coming a little bit closer to finding out what he is really like. I hope you can too.

Evangelism

I mentioned before how I went evangelising in the park with some of the youth group. It was a humbling experience. I would never dream of doing it. It would never ever cross my mind and if on the remote off chance it did cross my mind I would quickly stamp on it. When it was suggested my heart began to race, not with excitement, not because I found the idea thrilling. My heart raced in blind panic. The voices in my head stopped mid sentence and screamed NOOOOOOOOOOOOOOOOO! For a moment I tried to think of a plausible reason why it was a bad idea. None came. Stupid slow brain! I talked to Average Dave about this. He felt the same. When he heard what we were going to do, his heart sank. He said he wanted to do something fun and exciting. Interestingly, that is just what the kids thought it was. They looked like we were heading off to go white-water rafting on Saturn. They couldn't wait to get at it. It was me who was dragging my feet.

Once we got to the park though, things were so different. Dave and I cleverly created the role of prayer cover. The kids would do the talking and we would sit and watch and pray. This excited me. I wouldn't have to talk to anyone. Dave and I sat on the grass and prayed, and then he said exactly what I had hoped he wouldn't say.

"We should really go and talk to someone, shouldn't we?"

"I was just thinking that," I lied. I couldn't be the only one who didn't want to do this, could I?

A few seconds later we were sat on the grass chatting to a lovely couple in their 50s about God. The conversation flowed. They were genuinely interested in what we had to say. Dave did most of the talking. They talked about life, work and God with equal interest. We talked for a good 15 minutes. Dave challenged them to consider their destiny; they said they would. They had a friend who was a Christian. They decided to talk to him about all this.

We walked away, shocked. It had been so easy. It was just talking. I began to get excited. Why hadn't we done this before? It all seemed so obvious to me. This was what it was all about. We were here to tell people all about Jesus. Suddenly I was extremely keen.

"Guide us to the next person, God," I prayed out loud. A man reading caught our attention. Two on one. This would be even easier. We excused ourselves and sat down. We asked him some questions; he chatted openly. He asked some questions, and we answered. Then we talked about the bible. The man sat up a little and lifted his book. He was reading the *Oxford*

Companion to the Bible. I nearly jumped up and did a twirl, but decided against it as it would probably have killed the atmosphere a little and I didn't have my ballet slippers with me.

"Don't read anything into this, guys," he said. He was on to us, he knew were trying to brainwash him.

"So are you going to read it alongside the bible then?" Dave asked. "You really should."

"Yeah, I think I might," said our new friend. We made some small talk and a few minutes later we were leaving the park.

This has challenged my whole idea of things. If people are so open to talk about God why am I never bringing it up? We had two conversations in the park that day. Both were pretty positive experiences for everyone involved. We didn't see any fish jump on the hook, but they swam a little closer to the bait. It was so exciting. Hopefully we will go again soon.

There is real aversion to it though. So many of us in the church are not willing to tell other people. Dave did a talk at camp recently about evangelism. His main thrust was that we have got to bring up the subject of Christianity. There were a few leaders who were uncomfortable with that idea. Some even disagreed with it.

There was a genuine feeling that it is better to live a life that leads to questions rather than our choosing to make statements. I have issues with this.

We are treating Jesus like a shampoo. People look at our hair and are supposed to ask how we get it so shiny. "I use an anti-dandruff shampoo, I have dandruff," we answer.

"You would never guess," comes the reply. We expect people to look at our lives and ask how we get them so shiny. The fact is that I am yet to meet someone whose life is so shiny that they are worth asking the question.

Don't get me wrong. I like to see the good in people, and there are a lot of people who are doing much better than I am, but I have yet to meet someone who makes me want to ask about Jesus. We expect people to look at us and be amazed at our goodness and then ask us how to get good like us. To me, it seems like we are putting all the work of evangelism onto our own shoulders. It is meant to be the work of the Holy Spirit. I might even go so far as to say that the lack of success in evangelism in the past few years of my life has been down to my attempt to evangelise without saying the words. My life just hasn't been good enough to attract anyone to Christ – it never will be.

Maybe I'm not the only one. Maybe the church has fallen into the trap of trying to be so well behaved that the world starts asking it questions. Jesus continually did good things – and so should we – but he also preached. Over and over again, we read of Jesus going to the synagogues to preach and teach. What he said was backed up by what he did. He was far from a passive evangelist; he got people's backs up with the things he said. We worry so much about offending people these days. After all it's just not fashionable to be sure that what you believe is the final truth. I have so often said nothing out of fear of being labelled intolerant. But in this sense Christianity is intolerant. Our faith is held together by the fact that it is the sole way to God. I admit that there are ways and means of portraying this. There is a difference between being sure and being arrogant. I hope we can fall into the former rather than the latter.

Dave used an illustration of a blind man. Jesus liked to give sight to blind men, so for me it was almost biblical. Visualise a blind man walking along in the hills. He is enjoying the sounds and smells of the fresh air, the meadow. You notice though that he seems to know nothing of the cliff he is walking towards. You look around for his companion but he appears to be alone. You have to make a decision. What is the best thing to do? You decide to introduce yourself, start a conversation. He may ask you about the cliff after all, then it would all be okay. If he brings it up you'll tell him. You make some small talk, discuss the weather, some of the day's headlines. You offer him a drink, some food; you are friendly and encouraging. You begin to feel anxious though. You are getting closer to the edge. He hasn't brought it up. You begin to drop some hints, but he doesn't notice. Eventually you say goodbye and watch him walk on towards the edge. There was nothing you could do. He never brought it up. You couldn't bring it up – it might have offended him.

This is a bit of a ridiculous story, isn't it? It would never happen. No normally balanced person would allow another human being to walk off the edge of a cliff. It wouldn't be just. We are put on earth to look after each other. It is common decency to warn each other of danger. Except if that danger is hell. I am not a big fan of talking about hell, but it's real. The thought of challenging someone to consider that reality makes me feel ill, but the truth is our families and friends are in real danger of going there and for some reason completely unknown to me, I am more concerned about being laughed at or shouted down than about warning them. This should scare me. It should make me cry before God for their souls. What am I doing? If I claim to love these people as Jesus commanded me to, at least once in my life I should mention it. I don't have to be arrogant or rude. I am capable of lovingly communicating the realities of life. Advertising Jesus as a one-way ticket to paradise isn't the way. I am beginning to sound like some Texan fundamentalist but we have to be real: hell is as real as heaven. The choice is simple – one or the other. It's 100 per cent one way or the other. I am just not sure the church is offering people that choice. We are offering people a better life, money, successful marriages and a seat in heaven. People don't feel the need of salvation anymore because we have forgotten to mention what we all need saving from.

If we love people, we must speak. But we must also speak the truth, the whole truth in love. If we are serious about fulfilling our great commission we must do it all. We must live a life worthy of the name we have received, the name of Christ that we bear. We must love the poor; we must be honest, caring and patient. We must have time for our friends; we must sacrifice our needs for the needs of others. But we must also preach the whole gospel: we were all born headed for destruction; Jesus came to rescue us from the destruction of the world and the destination we were heading for. We need to remember the choice he has given us. Without him we had no choice; we had a non-negotiable destination. He has given us a chance. We know the secret, we must share it, and we must speak out. The world needs to hear it. How will they hear if no one tells them?

Repentance

I love those guys who wear sandwich boards with King James verses on them. I don't always agree with their method of evangelism but I love them just the same. I walked past a guy the other the day that wasn't satisfied with just a sandwich board but carried a 5-foot by 4-foot banner on two bamboo poles above his head. Both the sandwich board and the banner were plastered in badly painted slogans that can be summed up by the phrase, "God doesn't like you. Repent and he might think about it". As I said I don't begin to agree with the guy's methods but I love his passion. He is dying hard; every city has a few die-hard street preachers. Some use banners, some use megaphones, but they are in every city shouting at the masses. You have to love them; they have guts.

However, there are a few things I don't like about them. I have already mentioned that I feel many of them seem to take pleasure in the idea that those who don't turn will burn. That scares me to death. The other problem I have is that I think they have stolen something from me. It's not just them; there are others who are to blame. I'm not sure who started it, or when it happened, but someone somewhere formed a movement that has stolen one of the greatest gifts from the rest of us: repentance.

If you are like me, then you will have had the following experience. Imagine you are sitting in a church service and the preacher mentions the word repentance. If you are like me your mind immediately goes to someone else in the room. I hope they're listening to this, they need to hear it. I remember sitting down with friends after a sermon like this and discussing how it was so relevant for our friend who got drunk the night before. How we wished he had been there; he needed to repent. We can be such a bunch of idiots sometimes.

Another time I sat in a room of church leaders. I was to lead them in worship. We were praying for revival, so I turned to the revival verse, 2 Chronicles 7:14. In the middle of this call to us, the church, who are the people who are called by his name, we are told to turn from our wicked ways. We are told to repent. So I shared, that if we as the leadership of the church are serious about God hearing from heaven and healing our land, then we must lead the church in repentance. I could see people's discomfort. I prayed a prayer repenting of my ambition and my wanting to be known. A few others prayed but generally people weren't comfortable. In the days following there was a debate via email about whether or not I was right in what I had said. I never got involved in the debate, I was never asked to. I still think about that a lot. Maybe as you read you are remembering similar experiences, stories that you could share. These stories betray a hidden truth within the church.

We have lost the beauty of repentance. It has been slandered and abused to the point where we have rejected it. Repentance is a dirty word in the church. It is reserved for special occasions, for special cases. We keep it in a little tub in case we stumble across a notorious sinner who needs a dose. It's like the old bottle of milk of magnesia that came out when there was an emergency, crusted remnant round the lid from the last time we used it. When we actually use the word we apologise for it.

"Sorry for being politically incorrect, but tonight I want to talk about repentance." We call it old-fashioned, and every time we do the enemy laughs at us. He's convinced us to leave repentance gathering dust, along with hell and tithing and other dirty words. I suppose the enemy has also tricked us into believing repentance is an instantaneous thing; a one-off act at the point of salvation. We repent publicly of our sins at our baptism, or when we answer an altar call. In general though that is its last public appearance for most of us.

We have become uncomfortable with the idea. For a lot of my Christian life repentance hasn't been a part of my faith. I have never really allowed myself to feel in need of it. I guess it's because I view those who need to repent as weak, those who are immature in their faith. I have always considered myself as pretty mature. I don't need to repent – the smokers, drinkers and revellers do. The clubbers and the winos. Not me, I'm doing okay.

I have lost sight of its beauty. Repentance is the gateway to grace, the key to restoration and the fanfare of freedom. Repentance heralds the arrival of the most beautiful of God's ideas: grace. Grace we can handle: we lap it up, we bathe in it. We sing endless songs about it. The bestselling Christian books of the last ten years include at least two about grace. Repentance though, that's another story all together; it gets messy, honest. There's a bit too much grit about repentance. It makes us feel ill at ease. Unfortunately we can't have one without the other. I have a picture in my mind of a bottle of fine wine. It is no ordinary wine. It is heaven's wine, matured over eternity for just the right length of time. It is made from the grapes of the Lord's vineyard and harvested by the Master Vinedresser. He has just sent his Son into the dark cellar to bring us a bottle each. There's enough for everyone. We can have a bottle each, but a drop will change us forever. He gives us each a taste when we ask. It lights up our being. The Son hands us the bottles. We look at them, and some of us read the label. We hold it up to the sky to see its colours tint the sunlight red and green. It's beautiful. We begin to talk about the wine, what wonderful colours, what an amazing gift.

The Master Vinedresser reaches for a corkscrew and the mood changes. We cower back, clutching our bottles to our chests. We are happy with the wine in the bottle. Something so precious must be saved; it must be hoarded. We ignore the corkscrew. We scuttle off and form clubs to discuss the wine, the shape of the bottle, the colour and the cork. We write books about the wine, we sing about it. The wine is wonderful. One or two people go back for the corkscrew. They take it in their hands and look at its beauty. It is silver and gold and platinum, encrusted with precious stones. Its twists and turns reflect the sunlight in all the colours of the rainbow. It is a precious thing. In turn the handful of curious seekers take the corkscrew in their hands. They open the bottle, they smell the top. Their senses ignite once again with the aroma of grace. They pour, they gently swirl the red liquid in the ball of their glass. Then they taste the wonder of God's greatest gift. They receive the special reserve, held back for the victorious Son, the heir to God's throne. As they pour, the bottles remain full. They drink until their souls are overflowing with joy. There is an endless supply. They drink their fill.

We have only tasted grace; it has only wetted our tongues. We receive the cup of grace at salvation and celebrate it. So many of us take just enough to save us, when there is an endless supply to transform us. Salvation was never meant to be an instantaneous decision – it is dynamic and active. Somewhere post-Reformation we decided that we should pray the prayer of salvation and then on judgement day we walk away with Jesus' reward. It's true we will, but there is more to it than that. Salvation is for the now; we are saved now. We can experience the joy of our salvation in the daily mess of our lives. We are daily being saved from our sins. One prayer on the day of our conversion is enough to cover the lot, but there is so much more on offer.

Remember the lift we felt when we first followed Jesus, the lightness we felt in our souls when we knew our sins were forgiven? Where did it go? Why do so many of us feel eaten alive by guilt? Why are so many of us clothed in our shame? Aren't we free of this stuff? Didn't he promise us life to the full? Yet the church is full of fallen, broken people who are afraid to admit their fallenness and brokenness to themselves and to each other. Instead we bury it in our hearts until they overflow with hurt and guilt and shame. Our salvation is meant to be active, alive. Our salvation is meant to be a process as well as an instant. We can once again feel the lift, the unburdening. We can once again stand at the cross and have the weight of our shame lifted from our shoulders. When we come daily and offload our filth in repentance, and he daily replaces it with the wonder of grace, then we can experience this freedom.

Let's steal it back, let's take it out of the cupboard, dust it off, and polish it up. Let's put repentance back on display. The scriptures say there is rejoicing in heaven over one sinner who repents (Luke 15:7). Let that rejoicing be heard in the corridors of the church. Let us celebrate our freedom to repent, our freedom to trade ashes for a crown of beauty, sin for grace. Repentance is a gift to shout about.

Worship

Buzz word.

I was talking to a couple of friends the other day. We were talking about church. They had begun attending a new church recently. "What's it like?" I asked.

"It's good, the worship is fantastic," came the reply.

Again, as I am in the habit of doing, I smiled. I was pleased for them; they had found a church with good worship. Sitting here now though I am not sure what that means. What is "good worship"? I am a worship leader, I write worship songs, I have preached on worship, but I have little idea of how define good worship. I know what was meant in the conversation I had with my friends. We meant that a twenty-something with a £500+ guitar sang Matt Redman and Tim Hughes songs. We meant that there was space given between songs for reflection. There were spontaneous times of prayer and praise. The chorus would be repeated quietly then loudly during most songs. We meant that the sung praise time in their church's services would be about half an hour. People would raise hands; some would sit quietly and pray. I understand what we meant but I still don't know if that defines good worship.

I wonder when the word worship got hijacked. I wonder at what point the word worship was stolen by the Christian music industry. Who was first to describe their musical style as worship? Doesn't matter really, it's too late; we have already lost that word. It now means three chords, simple melody, sing-able lyrics. I'm not satisfied with that though. There is much more to it than that. Every so often when I am leading worship I pay lip service to the true meaning of the word. Worship is a lifestyle, not a half-hour on a Sunday. I say it but I don't live it. My friend Malcolm said something very true to me once. Malcolm inspires me to worship. His life is like mine: he struggles in things, he messes up daily, just like the rest of us, but he pursues God in worship. In a mini-van about 40 miles west of Chicago Malcolm hit on a truth that four years on I am still processing. Put simply, it is this: everything we can do that is not sinful should be an act of worship.

I expand on that idea in my mind and realise that if I am not worshipping God when I play sport then I am doing it for myself. I'm sure Jesus tells me to love God with all of my mind, body and soul. I don't come close. None of us really do. Can God really get glory from my eating a sandwich? Well of course he can.

I want to construct a list, a list of what I do. Two columns: on the left an *I-worship-with-these-things* column; on the right an *I-do-these-for-me* column. I can see it in my mind. It's pretty embarrassing. There are about three things on the left hand side: song, guitar and prayer. Maybe the longer I think about it, the more I can write in there. The thing is though, I am pretty normal. Most of us have a sparsely populated left column and an overcrowded right column. Eating, socialising, exercising – me, me, me. Entertainment, laughing, gardening – me, me, me. My mind is racing. What if I gave all these things over to worship? Imagine if I cut the grass for God. What a difference! Imagine if I cut the grass for his pleasure, not because of what the neighbours think. What about praising God for the fruit juice I drink as I drink it? Is it possible to find a life of worship that gives every instant for his glory? I'd love to have the stick-ability to do it for a week. I imagine the difference would be incredible. This isn't a new idea, Paul wrote it down a couple of thousand years ago.

"And whatever you do, whether in word or deed, do it all in the name of the Lord Jesus, giving thanks to God the Father through him." Colossians 3:17

That sounds like worship to me. That sounds like the proper response to God for what he has done. Much better than a few songs on a Sunday.

Many of us struggle to connect with these times. On many occasions I have stared at the words on a projector screen or in a Mission Praise songbook and been unable to sing them. They seem so far from where I am at. Pick a song at random from our church song list. There is a song we sing quite often that is packed with references to an undivided heart, or to being completely surrendered to Jesus. I find it so hard to sing. It's not true for me: my heart is divided; every Sunday I worship him with a divided heart. Am I alone? I don't think I am. I come Sunday after Sunday with a heart that is polluted with selfishness and pride. With 50 per cent of my heart surrendered, maybe 60 per cent at best, but never with all of my heart. Sometimes I sing my own words over the melodies. In this case I may sing "Jesus teach my heart to worship you." I take so much comfort from the Psalms. Pick a random Psalm…39.

Good choice. Psalm 39 finds David lamenting his anger. In verse 12 David describes how he feels like an alien with God, a foreigner, a stranger. The Psalms are full of honesty like this. They echo the cries of all humanity. They are full of failure and doubt, yet the pervading truth is God's faithfulness. I fear that we are losing touch with our honesty. Surely part of worshipping in spirit and in truth must be honestly admitting our failures. Rather than I-love-you songs, I need more I-want-to-love-you songs. I tried to write one yesterday. I feel silly though, like I am the only struggler but I'll take the risk and share it:

> Jesus I come to you,
> Broken in my sin and shame.
> What else can I do?
> You can make me new again.
>
> To know your love
> Is holding me,
> To know your grace
> Has covered me
>
> Is all I need.
> You're all I need.
> Everything you are is all I need.
>
> When I have fallen back,
> You lift me up again.
> When I can't walk at all,
> You love will be my strength.

It's true that so often I go to him as my last option. What else can I do? I have generally tried everything else before I admit that. I break myself so often with sin, but then forget to mention it as I sing I-love-you-Jesus songs. It's a sign of the times: failure is not an option; admitting it is even worse. But I figure that God knows where I have been all week. He has seen my behaviour and has heard my thoughts. He knows that to sing that my heart and life are his would be lies. I need to come as who I am. I need to bring him my sin and shame as well as my success. I believe that it is in the times when I worship him honestly that he gets the most pleasure. When I come as his child and tell him where I have been, what I have done and who I have hurt that he is blessed. I don't want to patronise him anymore with borrowed words and clichéd promises. I want to tell the truth – it's liberating.

I've been thinking about what James wrote. "Come near to God and he will come near to you." (James 4:8). I feel so much closer to him when I worship him honestly, when I bare my soul, when I show him my weaknesses as well as my strengths. I believe it brings him closer to me as well. I want to challenge myself to be more honest with him. I want to challenge those I fellowship with to be more honest. Let's write and sing songs that give honest praise. Words that are earthy and real, that fall on his mercy, the cries of broken clay in the hands of the Potter. When we do, I believe he will come again in power. He will heal us as we sing; he will restore us and fix us. Let us worship him with honest spirits in the truths of his grace.

My other struggle with "good worship" is that I make my decision based on how it makes me feel. If I leave a service feeling blessed or loved, then I will judge it as a good worship experience. Odd that. I thought it was all about him. I sometimes wonder how many of my "good" worship times have blessed his heart? How many times have I left a service feeling loved by him and forgotten to say I love him? Why are the worship songs I love the most centred on my wellbeing rather than his glory? Why do my hands go up and my eyes close when I sing lines that focus on my need? This to me has been good worship. Perhaps to him it is more like a musical shopping list.

Maybe not though. John Piper in *Desiring God* writes of a God who gets glory from our need of him. God has designed us with the clichéd, "God-shaped hole" to drive us to worship him. He has designed us with a deficiency that insists that we call out to him in our need. Perhaps we can go as far as saying that to need him, and ask for him to fill and bless us, is a key element to true worship. We need to overcome the misunderstanding that we cannot enjoy worship. We must learn to delight ourselves in him, make him our pleasure. It is then that he will come close, and it is then that we will bless his heart.

Acceptance

Sometimes I wish I had gone to school with Jesus. I would have loved to watch him at lunchtime. I can imagine who he would have sat with. I can see him sitting at the table with the smelly kid and the guy everyone called gay because of his voice. I can imagine him standing up against the school bully in defence of a tiny 11 year old. Other times though I am glad Jesus didn't go to my school. The reason, I remember what I was like at school. I was head of the Christian Union, I was known for being a Christian, and I was arrogant and cocky and a moral snob. If I had grown up with Jesus, he would have had a thing or two to say to me. I think of the tongue-lashings he gave the Pharisees when they took the moral high ground, "You brood of vipers," he said. I'm pretty sure I would have been on the end of some of those lashings had Jesus been in my form class.

Not much has changed either. I am just a little better at hiding my thoughts these days. I still don't like people who don't share my hobbies. I still have a hierarchy of sins. I find it much easier to accept my own judgementalism over someone else's swearing. I still find it easier to ignore someone who is being bullied than to stand up for them. But worse than that, I have constructed my own little set of rules by which I judge people's worthiness. If you fit my criteria, then you can be called a Christian. Sometimes I wonder why God allows me to stay alive. I live in the hope that he's teaching me something. Hopefully it's not how to avoid thunderbolts.

It's not even that God hasn't taught me the lesson a million times either. Let me tell you about Ken. I met Ken at about 6pm on 2nd January 2000. The date is relevant; I was in one of those resolution moods. This wasn't just New Year's resolution either this was New Millennium resolution. I had set my goals for how to love God more and how to love people more. The band I was in at the time, Joshua's Promise, were playing a gig in Belfast that evening. We had taken a break from sound check and half of us and another friend had headed to a burger bar for a healthy snack. As we walked up to the door a guy staggered out from behind a tree. "Let me tell you a joke, lads."

I can honestly say I was repulsed. I am ashamed of that, but all I could concentrate on was the smell, a mixture of stale cigarettes, alcohol and human filth. I wanted to run. I shaped my mouth for the words "no thanks" but before I got past the N, David our friend had stopped, leaned against the tree and said, "Sure go ahead."

David's newfound friend continued to tell us a joke about tarmac, a bar and one for the road. It's in my top five bad jokes, but David laughed. I think it was at this point that God began to do something in me. I can remember a battle going on in my mind. I started to have a disconcerting love for Ken swell up in my chest, and then it would be extinguished sensibly by my head. This went on for a few minutes as David talked to him.

I began to ask God to help me love Ken. The struggle subsided and my chest won the fight. Before I knew what was happening I had bought Ken a meal in a local restaurant and we were all sitting round a table talking. I had forgotten that he was so smelly. Part of me thinks God numbed my senses. People gave us weird looks, I felt embarrassed but I knew God was doing something so I stuck it out.

"So why are you guys in Belfast tonight? Here for the booze and ladies?" Ken asked while chewing a chip.

"No, we're here with a Christian band", I said, the first time I had spoken to Ken directly.

What happened next still tears me up. Ken's whole face changed. His eyes filled up. "You're Christians. So am I. I became a Christian in 1977. I was in hospital. I had been shot by the

IRA the night before." Ken pulled back his collar and showed us bullet wounds in his neck. One of the other band members put his finger in the hole.

"My life has been a nightmare, lads. I was shot again in 1980. I haven't been able to handle what has happened me. I have lost my wife, my son, my home. I was hit by car last week. I have been stabbed. I have been an addict and an alcoholic. There are people who have wanted me dead. I have run and run my whole life. But I'll never forget something I read in the bible the night I became a Christian in that hospital ward. Jesus says no one can get me out of his hand."

Ken, now with tears streaming, lifted a penny and illustrated for us with more power than any preacher, what Jesus meant when he uttered the words of John 10:28.

"This penny is me, lads," Ken took the penny and laid it on his greasy palm. Closing his fingers over the penny he looked me in the face and said, "and Jesus is never letting me go. He never has yet." About an hour later Ken was gone and we were surrounded by polite middle-class Christians. I couldn't help but wondering who knew God best.

Ken would never have made it into a church. He would have been evicted before he reached the top step. His problems would have discounted him from a welcome. Christians don't behave like him, do they? The truth is they shouldn't, I know that, but I have no doubt that God's grace will save Ken through faith as much as it will save me. Ken is church as much as Billy Graham is church, as much as the apostle Paul is church. You and I are church as much as these three. Despite our sins and our inconsistencies we are welcome. We are accepted by Jesus into his church. When are we – when am I – going to learn to accept people as unfinished works? I expect people to accept me as I am, but I find it so much harder to return the favour. I want to find the rulebook that someone drew up years ago that decides who is welcome in church. It's probably unwritten, a secret verbal code spoken from generation to generation to stop people like me finding it and burning it. I pray that God will purge us of it. I pray he will renew our view of each other.

One my great heroes said two things that I feel are relevant. The first was this: where there is life there is mess. Dead things keep things tidy. That's true; the church should be messy, and the messy people should be most welcome, because it was with messy people that God has done his greatest work. Secondly, when asked about his high view of Mary, he said something like this. "Perhaps some people view her too highly. She was just another human. They shouldn't pray to her but we need to ask ourselves this. Do we view other humans too lowly?"

I guess what he meant was this. Maybe some people do hold Mary a little too high in their theology, but we treat everyone else with much too little respect. Maybe, just maybe, these cracked clay jars we call Christians are filled with the treasure of God's own Holy Spirit, bursting out through the cracks, to change our tiny little worlds. Maybe if I learn to accept people's cracks as much as I want their treasure, I will see God more, I will meet him more. I'm pretty sure I will.

So what do we do about it? I guess I am committing to two things: the first is a change in my own heart. I pray that God will make me slow to judge and quick to love. Peter says that "love covers over a multitude of sins" (1 Peter 4:8). I want a love for people that stops me noticing. I want to see the beauty in people before I notice their shortcomings. I want my eyes to show love rather than contempt, my face to smile rather than grimace. I want people to feel the love of Jesus when they meet me. I want them to notice their own beauty and ignore their own failings because of my look. I believe that is how Jesus was. He loved people so purely, so fully that they forgot who they were. They felt whole again in his presence. I'll take some of that, I would love to do that for just one person.

Secondly, I am committing to defend the slandered. I pray for the guts to defend the objects of people's criticism. We must banish this from the church. The body of Christ cannot house the habit of gossip. It is divisive and will lead us to more pain. We must learn to heal rather than scourge the sinful.

"Please, God, grant us this gift. Make us more like your perfect Son. Amen."

Prayer

I remember once seeing a little book in a friend's bathroom. It was entitled something like *The Prayers of Five Year Olds*. It was one of those little books you buy someone for their birthday when you can't think of anything else. It consisted of about 30 short prayers written by five-year-olds. They ranged from the heart wrenching prayers asking God to look after a dead bunny to the silly. There were some amazing ones. The one that stood out to me went something like this.

"Dear God, please don't let me have to sit beside Danny in school tomorrow. I don't like him. Love, Harry"

That's honesty for you. Not only did the kid pray it, he had it printed in a little book for other people to pray with him in bathrooms all over the world. It's good though, to be honest like that when we pray.

I compare the prayers of these kids, ("please God can I have a red car like Billy's?", "please God can I be a princess?") with the prayers you and I pray at church. So often it feels so clinical, so contrived. There are key elements that we need to include or else it won't count. In one church I attended I am sure there were rules about rhythm. You had to pray as if you were on a rollercoaster. Up and down, up and down. Fast then slow for dramatic effect. The phenomenon is hard to describe in words. It has to be demonstrated, but if you have experienced it you know exactly what I am talking about. It's almost as if by dramatising certain phrases God would be more convinced to answer. Those same people spoke in very different ways when the got excited about football or a new car. Where did this strange prayer rhythm come from? I quite often wonder whether or not I pray in a funny voice in public. Maybe we all do.

Prayer is a funny thing really. It's got to be one of the easiest things in the Christian life to do, but the thing that most people say they struggle with. I have so many conversations with people about how we find it hard to pray. We say things like, "I just feel like I am talking to the ceiling" and "After about five minutes I begin to drift off into a daydream." Then we get round to talking about the little gimmicks we have that help us pray. Lists and calendars and acrostics. Then there are those cards that we keep in our bibles and wallets to remind us of things. Very few of these things seem to help though. Actually I find that they make me feel guiltier. I look at the prayer list or calendar a couple of months later when I find it in a bible or book I've been reading and realise that I have prayed for about one thing on the list. I have begun to avoid those lists. I also don't like to write them for other people.

Sermons on prayer are interesting as well. They usually contain that quote from Wesley (although I have head it attributed to both Luther and Calvin as well; it depends on your theology as to who said it). "If I have a particularly busy day, I must pray for two extra hours to get me through it." The sermon ends with the finger wagging statement, PRAY MORE! Wow, that's deep! We all go home from church and by Monday we slip back into our routine. There is definitely a biblical precedent for coming aside from the world and spending time in prayer. If we follow Jesus' example, it was generally early in the morning. This makes it even more difficult. On goes another layer of guilt: I can't even get up early enough to pray properly.

I am encouraged by Paul's call to pray without ceasing. Pray at all times, pray in all things. Always be in prayer. That seems more possible to me. Two or three hours solid seems so hard, seems like such a stretch. Two or three hours throughout the day though, I can do that. In fact I reckon I do do that.

Joanne and I went to Wales a few months ago. I was preaching at a men's breakfast in a little Welsh village called Crosshands where our friends Simon and Emma live. Crosshands is exactly half way between Swansea and Carmarthen. It was the site where the prisoners from Swansea jail were handed over to the guards from Carmarthen jail and vice-versa. The little church there that we were visiting sits up on a hill over the village. It was a wonderful weekend. Simon and I talked late into both nights we stayed there. We talked about God, church, many of the things I am writing about now. He said a little catchphrase that really blessed me. He described me as a person who rarely prays for twenty minutes but prays every twenty minutes. I remember hesitantly agreeing and Simon saying "that's all right!" You know I think he might be right; perhaps it is okay to pray like me. I do my best to involve God in all my decisions and when I am really doing well I even listen to what he wants me to do.

I find a certain freedom in this idea. That it is all right that I don't pray for a long block every day because I do pray a lot during the day. Sometimes I get up early and pray for an hour. Sometimes I go for a walk or a drive and pray as I travel. Most days I have this kind of drawn-out conversation with God. I find myself looking at people and praying for them. I ask God questions, I sing sometimes. When I am alone in the house I talk to him, even when I watch television. I pray in the bath, as I lie in bed. I actually pray quite a lot. Are these valid prayers? Yes. Are they less valid that the prayers of the people who are up at the crack of dawn on their knees? I don't think so.

I don't want to suggest that we stop committing chunks of our lives to prayer. As I said, Jesus did that and so it is good that we do. The times we spend praying for two or three hours can really bless us and refresh us and quite often that is when things are achieved in prayer. We should continue to try and pray at length. But we mustn't feel guilty when we don't manage it. I don't think I am alone in the way I pray. I think a lot of people pray the way I do.

I sat in prayer meeting recently with a group of leaders who prayed for God to direct them in how they should reach the lost. After half an hour or so there was a time set aside to listen to what God had to say. I felt pretty strongly that God was asking us to stop the way we do things and wait on him. In the groups we were involved in leading we needed to stop and wait in prayer. I shared this as I thought I should. A lot of people agreed and added their feeling that this was what God was saying. A few people prayed and asked God to show them the specific things they needed to stop. Afterwards in conversation with a couple of the men who were there I was told something that really worried me.

"Dave, we come here to pray. We don't come here for direction. We can get direction at the churches and groups we are from. We just come here to pray."

Being a young man is very difficult for me sometimes. I am learning slowly to keep my mouth shut about things. This was one time I managed not to say something stupid. That conversation really worried me. How can we pray week after week after week for God to guide and save, and then ignore what he says? What is the point in asking for directions if you are going to ignore them? I have done that before; I stopped once in America and asked for directions to a nearby town. The directions the local gave me didn't seem right to me so I ignored them. Guess what? I got lost. I'm pretty sure though that the meeting I am talking about is just one place where this is happening. If we pray for direction, it will come. It must. James tells us that if we ask for God's wisdom he will give it. Why are so many of us praying and not listening for the direction? Or, even worse, hearing it and denying it? The Israelites did that the whole way through the bible and each time the result got worse. Eventually they ended up in exile. The Jews prayed for a messiah for hundreds of years. When he came he didn't look like God's Chosen One so they got right back to praying. I think this is why prayer gets so dry sometimes.

The biggest church in the world is in South Korea. It has around 750,000 active members. The pastor there was asked his strategy by an American church growth specialist.

"Well our strategy is twofold," replied the pastor, "we pray and obey."

The people I know whose prayer lives are exciting and vibrant are the ones who pray with that strategy: that God will direct them and if they obey his directions, answers will come. Whether for two hours in the morning or spread through out the day, we must pray and expect an answer back. Otherwise I am not sure what the point is.

Identity

I've just come back from Alex's office. Alex is on fire. Jesus fills his chest and mixes with the air in his lungs. When Alex talks about Jesus you see his whole being swell. There is something intimidating about someone who is that in love with Jesus. There is also something beautiful. It draws you to a person.

Somewhere in amongst the boyish banter and the in-jokes, we talked briefly about how we are considered pure and holy by the Father through the shared riches of Christ. In reality, in factual reality, the Father looks at us and considers us worthy of Christ's riches. I wish my mind would deal with that. I wish something in my subconscious would click into place and I would catch a glimmer of what it means to be considered a co-heir with Christ. I long to understand how the Father looks at me and sees me as one with Christ. How I can be clothed in his righteousness and counted as pure and holy in the sight of the Father? It is beyond my feeble imagination. It is a wonder; it is a mystery.

It is a mystery because I live with me. I hear the things I mutter under my breath sometimes. I know the thoughts I replay in my head. I know the impatience and the wandering. I know the weakness and the irrationality. I taste my lukewarm life firsthand and, instead of spewing it out and longing for the heat of a life dominated by him, I comfort myself in the innocuousness of it all.

I know who I am, but I refuse to accept who I am in him. I choose regularly to walk in my old clothes. Worn and torn, soiled and stained by my sin and unreliability, I leave my garment of praise and grace in the wardrobe and languish in the rags of my desires. It disturbs me to put the truth down on paper. Writing this is making me aware of something I have denied.

Four weeks ago we had a youth workers' prayer meeting. We met at the local Salvation Army citadel. Derrick had fashioned a huge 24-7 prayer room. We used it for our meeting. At one point we split up and spread amongst the numerous stations within the room. In the centre of the room was a tent. It had a curtain across the middle, separating front from back. It represented the Most Holy Place. The curtain was torn down the middle.

I chose to sit on the far side of the curtain in the Most Holy Place. I lay on my back and stared at the canvas roof of the tent. I prayed. I sat in silence. My mind began to move to the symbolism of the place. Here I was lying face up in the presence of Almighty God. I rolled over and lay face down. It was painful. If I moved too quickly, my knees and hips ground on the hard floor. I was uncomfortable. I don't lie face down too often. I stuck it out though. After about ten minutes of uncomfortable contemplation, a thought came to me. Every day I can choose to walk in the manifest presence of God Almighty. The Spirit of the Living God is with me daily. I can choose to live in accordance with his will, to live face down, or I can choose my own way, my own selfish pursuit of pleasure. It is painful to live in the presence of God. It hurts. We face things we would not face if we chose our own way. We are attacked and rejected. We wrestle with our own thoughts and we choose others over ourselves. The blessing that comes from sticking it out is beyond compare though. I cannot imagine the pleasure I will feel if I enter heaven to the greeting "well done, good and faithful servant".

Another thing I hear Alex say quite often is this: "there is nothing good in me but him. I know how sinful I am, but in him I am holy." That has got to be very freeing. He says it with such passion and conviction that you know he is living that truth. It is something I have lost along the way. I have lost track of the fact that I am also free in Christ, an adopted son of the Most High. It is liberating to consider the consequences of such a truth. Nothing I do, nothing I think, nothing I say can take away my sonship. For it is not of me; it is all of him. I can run for eternity and feast on my sin, and yet he still will call me his child. It is all of Jesus; it is nought of me. My identity is wrapped in his, woven into the fabric of his being, and it would take time beyond eternity to unravel it.

These are the badges of my life, these the emblems of who I am – a son, a child, an heir. These are the adjectives of my being – holy, chosen, accepted. My shirt is righteousness and my jacket praise. As I walk through York and get on with the mess of life and the day-to-day, this is who I am.

This is who we are, but you and I both choose another way. We choose an altogether more cumbersome existence. We carry the weight of our past and the guilt of our present on our backs. We stitch the badges of our failures on our arms like wayward and confused boy scouts. We stitch them not in pride but in confusion. We have forgotten where to go with these things. We can go to him and trade ashes for a crown.

There is a verse hidden in Revelation. In among the dragons and the beasts there is a verse that talks of a white stone and a new name. The bible is big on new names: Abram Abraham, Jacob Israel, Simon Peter, Saul Paul. Each of these received a new name after an encounter with the Lord. I wondered why for a long time. Why was it so important that Simon became Peter and Saul, Paul? I think I know now. I am happy to be proven wrong by a wiser theologian.

Before he met Jesus, Simon was known by at least a few people. His name had become synonymous with his life, his temperament, his work. Simon son of John: the fisherman, the quick-tempered, the volatile. That is the picture we paint of Simon these days. On meeting Jesus Simon changes completely. He becomes Peter the loyal, and the leader of the church. He is no longer as volatile; he is secure, a rock, a stone among the foundations of the church. If we drew a timeline of Simon's conversion to becoming Peter, we would see a marked change after his three-year encounter with Christ. He is a changed man.

Saul is the same. Abram, Jacob. All are changed when they encounter the Lord. The name changes were not an aesthetic choice of the Creator. They were necessary; they became different people. Their names were no longer bound up in who they were; they had new lives, new purposes, new identities.

If we each took a piece of paper and wrote the things we reckon people think of when they hear our names, the lists may upset some of us. Many of us would write things that were quite negative. We would remember the people we have let down and the labels people have stuck on us in jest. My list would read like this: unreliable, grumpy, unfit, foreign, attention seeker, under-qualified, too young, too old etc, etc. I could fill this page. Don't feel sorry for me, I reckon I am normal. I think many other people would have similar lists.

I like to do this exercise with young people. I give them a page and ask them to write their name at the top. I ask them to then define their name using the feelings they have about themselves and the things they think other people think of them. They fill their page and then I ask them to tear it up. I then give them another blank page. Again they write their name at the top. Again they define their name. This time they write God's thoughts though. I help them using scripture. I guide their minds through their identity in Christ.

The effect this can have on some people is dramatic. For the first time they consider themselves forgiven instead of sinful, chosen instead of rejected. The Holy Spirit gently reminds them of who they are in Christ.

This is how we receive our new name. The definition of who we are changes. When the Lord hears our name, we are no longer sinful and shamed – we are accepted and loved. He has redefined us and reordered our identity.

The white stone is another thing. I am told by a reliable source that in the days when Revelation was written, certain rich men invited guests to their banquets by sending them an engraved white stone. We are each given a white stone inviting us into the courts of heaven. Our name is engraved on it, our new name, the name that inherits the riches of Christ. We are called to a feast, we are guests of honour, the Bride of Christ, we are welcome at the banqueting table of the Living God. That is an identity I am proud to bear.

The Cross

About two weeks ago my colleague James and I were clearing out our storeroom. It is a room about six feet by four feet. It is full of all sorts of wonders and delights ranging from books to dressing up gear. I spent at least part of the day wearing a plastic Viking helmet. It didn't quite fit but looked great with the blonde plaited wig I found.

After the fun and games died down, I placed the helmet on top of my computer monitor. It sat there for a week. Eight days after I put it there we were right in the middle of our prayer and gift week at church. James was being really holy and praying a lot. He went a few times to the Minster to pray. Most days I managed about twenty minutes. On one occasion while James was out at the Minster I put on some worship music, and prayed a little. After about ten minutes my eyes fell on the Viking helmet. Immediately into mind came the thought that I should take it down from there. I took it down but again I had a strong feeling. I felt that I should place a cross above my desk. I should work under the shadow of the cross.

I got up and went to the storeroom. I found an old bamboo cane, some string and a junior hacksaw. In about ten minutes I built a crude cross. I took some sticky tack and stuck it above my desk. It is still there. As I stuck the cross on the wall, I had a thought that knocked me back onto my seat. I don't 100 per cent if it was God speaking to me, but it felt like it was.

"In the same way you made this bamboo cross, the cross of Christ was fashioned for you."

I felt my spine crush under the weight of that truth. The cross of Christ was carved and nailed together, rough as it may have been, because of me. The Son of God, Jesus Christ was nailed onto two pieces of wood and hung naked before the world, despised and rejected because of me.

Two things happened in my head at the same time. I wanted to rejoice and thank God for his love, but I was broken by my lack of love for him. I was reeling for a long time afterwards. My life in no way reflects a gratitude for what Jesus has done for me on the cross. In no way whatsoever do my attitudes, thoughts and actions suggest that I have any real understanding of what the cross was all about.

I grew up with a picture of the crucifixion in my mind. It was of a beautiful man, a handsome man with a beard, arms spread, hanging on a perfectly carved piece of wood. There was nothing disturbing about that image; it didn't haunt my thoughts. Again I worry that I am not the only one with this image in my head. In my head Jesus was almost smiling as he took the sin of the world on his soul and the viciousness of man on his body. These images in my head rarely portrayed suffering, rarely portrayed the absolute horror that was the reality of the scene on Good Friday. They were more akin to the illustrations of a children's bible. They were though much easier to accept.

These images were destroyed the day I went with my brother to watch Mel Gibson's movie *The Passion of the Christ.* I left the cinema feeling bruised. I felt beaten, disoriented and confused. I saw myself in the eyes of the soldiers, in the eyes of the scoffers. It was you and I who stood round and watched. I ran with Peter, I denied I knew him.

The cross began to gain a greater reality for me. For me Jesus rode by donkey into the city that within days would turn on him. For me he stayed silent at supper and didn't expose Judas. For me he cried in the garden as his friends fell asleep. For me he was betrayed by a friend's kiss. For me he was arrested and dragged through the city streets. For me he was slapped and spat on, mocked and scorned. For me he stood silent before his accusers. For me he was stripped naked and shamed before men. For me he was scourged, skin torn from muscle, muscle from bone. Each crack of the whip igniting his body with a piercing agony I cannot imagine. For me he was rejected instead of Barabbas. For me he walked the streets under the weight of a cross. For me he was nailed to that cross. For me he was hung in the air and left to rot in the heat. For me he was mocked and ridiculed. For me blood flowed down mingled with love. For me his Father turned his face away. For me the sin of the world was heaped on the Son of God. For me it is finished. For me he breathed his last. He died for me.

All of the imagery of Mel Gibson's movie came back to me as I sat in my office looking at two pieces of bamboo and a yard of string. I began to wince in my chair. I could feel my cheeks turn pale. I felt sick. This was all real, it really happened. I knew it was real but I had cleaned it up for myself. I felt ashamed. My life in no way reflected the knowledge I had of what Christ has done for me.

I prayed and repented of my lack of commitment, my wavering, wandering heart. I repented of my lack of concern for the lost who walk in and out of my life every single day. I wrote a prayer of commitment to God and stuck it up on the wall beside the cross. It read:

> May I remember your cross as if I built it with my own hands.
> May I remember your scars like I drove nails into flesh.

May I remember your blood like I
pierced your side.
May I remember your wounds like I
scourged your back.
May I remember your torment like I
mocked you aloud.
May I remember your pain like I broke
your heart.
May I remember your tomb like I buried
you dead.
May I remember your resurrection like I
saw its first light.
May I never forget what you have done
for me.

I have begun to wonder how it must have been for the disciples. They actually saw it happen. They had eaten and walked and talked with Jesus for three years. They had touched him and knew his humour. They had been there when he had broken bread. Then they had seen him suffer and die and rise from the dead. I wonder if any of them ever really fully comprehended what had happened or if they lived the rest of their lives shaking their heads in wonder?

What must it have felt like seeing your best friend treated that way despite his innocence? What must it have felt like knowing that you were helpless to stop it? What must it have felt like to hold his mother as she wept uncontrollably while her son was torn to pieces by men with the dignity of rabid dogs?

I have heard people who appear shocked at the disciples' courage and achievements when they read of their exploits after Jesus departed. I have heard people marvel at their bravery and their perseverance. I don't marvel at it. They had an experience that would disturb even the weakest soul to courage. They had seen the Son of God submit to the hands of murderous men, all because he loved them to death. Loved them beyond death and loved them into eternal life. These eleven men and hundreds and thousands, perhaps millions after them understood the cross, understood what it meant for them and they were never the same again. I pray that the Lord will grant me a glimpse of the reality of what it means to preach Christ crucified. I want the passion of the eleven. I want to walk in the confidence that if it came to it I would stand firm in the knowledge of the cross.

Friendship

Outside my family, there are seven guys in the world who really know me. I would call any one of them a best friend and would be honoured to have anyone one of them return the favour. I can be myself in their company. I can be tired, grumpy, silly or honest. They accept me. One is Average Dave. I have known him the shortest time out of all seven, but he still makes the list. The others are known by some as the JPs, Joshua's Promise, the band we were in when we were students. These seven guys, the JPs and Average Dave, have taught me what it means to be a friend.

I have always had a vaguely romantic, poetic view of friendship. Friends have always seemed like the companions God gives us to make memories with. Friends fill the memories of our digital cameras, the chorus of our stage-show lives. I am blessed more than I can describe to have so many amazing friends. I have been surrounded by wonderful, honest people for as long as I remember, surrounded by people who have shaped me into who I am and will shape me into who I will become. They are tools in God's hands to re-create me into his likeness.

I have just come back from Malcolm's wedding. Malcolm is one of the JPs. He married Lucy in a beautiful country church, on a beautiful day in beautiful Northern Ireland. JP weddings are great times for me and difficult times as well. They are a chance to celebrate a friend's joy, and watch him enter into his life with his new bride. They are also great because I get to see the guys. Having moved to England the chances to see all six at once are few and far between. I guess from here on in it will be a bigger effort. We are running out of potential weddings to meet at.

A strange thing happened in my mind at Malcolm's stag meal. I was round a table with the guys and began to wonder whether they actually liked me. They weren't acting any differently than usual, but somewhere in the back of my mind came a doubt that they tolerated me but didn't like me. This was a new experience for me. I had always been pretty confident in relationships and had never before doubted the love these guys had for me. Within seconds though, I was looking round the restaurant and at the guys sitting in front of me. I began to realise that I was just one of many. I was just another person who gets up every morning and presents himself to the world in the hope that someone will like him. I get up every day with the other six billion people on earth who crave acceptance from each other. The conversation caught my attention and moved through food, football, Lord of the Rings and music. The thought clawed in the back of my mind though and returned later as I tried to sleep.

I thank God that he accepts me, I really do. I think I understand about 30 per cent of what it means to be accepted by God, but for what I can fathom I am thankful. There is something within me though that craves the acceptance of my peers. I notice it when I miss a joke, or when I'm late (this happens often). I notice it when I can't share in a memory of a group of friends. I want to be part of other people's lives and I want them to be a part of mine. I want to be a treasured friend, a confidant. I believe to these guys that I may be; they certainly are that to me. God made us for this. He built us for community, for friendship. Close, painful, life-changing friendship, primarily with himself and secondly with each other. He knew what he was doing when he made more than one of us. He built us with a need to be together, to work off each other, to learn from each other.

I believe that I carry a little piece of each of the JPs around with me. I think we are committed as a group to the betterment of each other. Each of them inspires me to better myself. Malcolm has a strength and honesty that shock me. Davy has a generous heart of patience that will give again and again with no return. Andrew has a passion to serve those around him. Aaron has a relentless heart chasing after God's own. Neil is committed to living a holy lifestyle no matter the cost. Jose has a creative and thoughtful mind that opens the truth up in a new light. When I am with these six guys I leave wanting to be better. I carry seeds of their passions in my heart. I see their fruit and want to graft them into the boughs of my life. They inspire me.

In the bible these relationships are described as iron sharpening iron. The picture is of two strong objects chipping equal parts off each other until both are perfectly sharpened. God provides us with men and women around us who chip parts off, sometimes painfully, sometimes gently. We become sharper the more we are around them. Sometimes I get lethargic and blunt; my heart bleeds for time with my friends. I am feeling that wound opening a little today, the day after Malkie's wedding. I miss the guys, I miss the laughs and the fun and the memories. There are more to come though.

In the bible there are many great friendships. I have always been fascinated by Jesus and Peter. To me they seem such opposites. I read Jesus as contemplative, gentle and controlled. I read Peter as headstrong, obstinate and more than a little impulsive. I see their relationship as more than a little one-sided at times. Jesus always seems to be giving to Peter and Peter seems more than happy to lap up his gifts. Peter makes some crazy mistakes. Jesus cries, "get behind me, Satan" after one of Peter's remarks. I often wonder why Jesus bothered. Woven into the story are some clues to his reasons. Peter recognises Jesus as the Christ before anyone else. Peter takes the risk of walking on water. Peter leaps to Jesus' defence. I have begun to realise that the relationship wasn't one-sided at all. Jesus gained something from Peter's friendship. Jesus was blessed by having Peter around. Sure, Jesus perfected what it meant to be a friend, but Peter in his stumbling, stammering humanity blessed the heart of Jesus and earned the name Rock – reliable, steady, Rock.

I guess I love the friendship of Jesus and Peter because I always feel like I can relate to Peter, John I am not so close to. He seems a little too good at getting it right for me. I relate more to Peter because I make his mistakes. Over and over again in the friendship I have with Jesus I do exactly what Peter did and worse. I have the hindsight of knowing Jesus rises again, but I still deny him by silence and action. I still run from the fire into the cool of anonymity. I still sink when I look at the waves. I still cut off the innocent's ear in an attempt to defend him at the wrong time, in the wrong way. I am blessed that Peter comes through to be a leader of the church, its foundation stone. I stood in his basilica in Rome and marvelled at the fact that the one who denied Jesus ended up with such a magnificent monument. My mind wandered to fanciful things that day: St Dave's Basilica, a monument to the one who denied Jesus, who sank in the sea, who ran away. I can be an egotistical little man.

My friendships with these seven guys reflect so clearly the friendship I have with God. I don't call them enough. I can be disloyal and rude. I can let them down. They stick around though, just like he does. They give second, third and fourth chances, and I take them. They receive the same from me. The reason? We have an unspoken understanding of a biblical principle. A chord of three strands is not easily broken. How about a chord of eight?

Love

When I was about seven we played a game where the loser's punishment was to tell the worst girl in school that you loved her. If you lost, you were teased for weeks about the fact that you loved that girl. There was a whole set of rhymes and chants that developed to ridicule the loser. I can't remember what the game was although I have a disturbing suspicion it involved peeing the highest. Boys really are strange when they are young; obviously we all grow out of such childishness by the time we are 18.

I remember chatting with a teenager once who had fallen into sexual sin with someone she had been with for a long time. She had been manipulated by that most twisted phrase, "if you love me, you will," the phrase that tricks young people into so much hurt. I remember asking her if she loved the guy. The reply was crushing. "I loved him with everything I had; I had nothing left to prove it other than my virginity." This girl's love was so strong for that idiot that she gave everything to prove it to him. He never believed her; he never would have. Love was unimportant, disposable, as long as he had sex with her. I never saw that girl again; I can't even remember where I spoke to her. My guess is that it took a long time before she loved a boy again. Her love was damaged and fragile. It needed some time before it could work again.

Hopefully she met someone, someone big and tough who could go and crush that other worm of a guy.

The reason I share these stories is to give two illustrations of what is happening in our world. The most precious of things is being abused. It is being used as a weapon against people to make them feel small. In the playground little kids like I was make the girl who doesn't fit in feel unlovable by joking that no one could ever love her. Young men and women are being manipulated into situations they don't want to be in by people who know the power that love can have over someone. There are countless other examples that portray love like a mistreated animal, fearful and rash, lashing out at anyone who comes near. Love is no longer a masterpiece hanging in the Louvre; it is a crumbling canvas sold to the highest bidder on *Bargain Hunt*. Memories of what it once meant to be in love are fading fast and are being replaced by convenient relationships and casual sex.

Actually I don't think that's true. I am forgetting something. This soiling and abusing of love is nothing new. Love has always been this way. It has been tainted since the Fall. Since the first loving relationship was tainted by selfishness, love has been a mess. Adam and Eve had it so good. They had everything they needed. They had more than they needed.

They existed in this relationship with the Creator that every being has yearned for ever since. They walked and talked and laughed with God. The bible describes the three of them walking through the Garden of Eden in the early evenings. My mind races with colours and glimpses of God's pleasure as they look at his creation together. I can picture the excitement on the faces of Adam and Eve as God arrives each evening to give them another tour of his world, the world that he had given to them. I imagine that at the end of their walks they will hug and slap high fives and have one last joke together before sleeping. Every time I think about that I get excited, because that's how I hope heaven is.

God had given Adam and Eve everything he had. He had allowed them right into the centre of his love. They had the most intimate communion that any created being has ever had. They had his love in all its tangible physical greatness. They could touch him and see him smile. They could hear the delight in his voice as he said their names. I would love just an afternoon of it, or even just a glimpse.

But, just like you and I, Adam and Eve wanted more and, just like you and I, they took the enemy's bait and stained their love forever. They cheated on God with his greatest foe. They sold their innocence for an empty promise and sacrificed the greatest prize for nothing. Since the day they took that fruit and ate it human love has been tainted in selfishness and sin. It feels almost completely gone at times.

The effects of their decision are being played out all over the world right now. Children are starving as rich people like me look on and feel sorry for them. My love stretches to a sigh and a sinking feeling but not to action. In Northern Ireland there were many people fighting for a cause they loved more than their fellow human beings. When Hurricane Katrina hit New Orleans in 2005 reports came through that hundreds of innocent people stranded by the floodwaters were assaulted and raped, as love for oneself became the only reason for living. It really does get depressing.

The bible tells us that "love never fails." When I look at the love that is being advertised on this earth, the self-love, the selfish-love, I wonder how that can be true. I almost worry that love is on its last legs. Then I begin to remember little tales of redemption that just make it out from the mess.

I read *Bono on Bono* recently. It's the first book of its kind I have ever read. I loved it. One thing that struck me was the references he made to the forgotten face of the war on poverty. He mentions men and women who feed AIDS orphans to the neglect of themselves. The one thing that stood out the most was the story of a man in Africa who begged Bono to take his son. He understood that his son had more chance of a life with Bono than he had if he stayed with his father. Here was a father whose son was the only joy he had left, yet he would give up everything he had to allow his son a chance. I read stories like that and begin to realise that love is very much alive. It is just shy; love by its very nature is shy.

I don't mean shy in the self-conscious sense, I mean shy in the deference of attention from one person to another sense. True love, pure love speaks powerfully in a quiet voice and when it speaks it lifts up the name of others, drawing attention away from itself.

I read an article once that I can't lay my hands on to quote properly. It was talking about the Trinity. The line that caught my attention spoke of the divine dance of love between the three members of the Godhead. I thought that picture was beautiful. The article gave examples of Jesus' love for his Father. In all Jesus did he was submitting in love to his Father. Jesus deferred attention to his Father. His love for his Father was so infinitely strong that he gave everything to him. The writer went on to describe the activity of the Holy Spirit, giving all glory to the Son and to the Father, and of the Father and

Spirit both giving glory to the Son on the day of Jesus' baptism.

I was excited to read of a love that is driven by a desire to hold the glory of another above the glory of oneself. We are called to love one another with this godly other-seeking, other-centred love. We are called to love in shyness. We are called to a love that defers attention away from us and puts attention on others. It is by this love that the world will know we are His.

The love shown in the bible is so different from the love I experience and the love that I practise. The love David had for God led to David's shame as he danced naked, lost in admiration for his king. The love of Abraham for God led to his sacrifice of all he had, even the willingness to sacrifice his only son. The love of Stephen led to his stoning, choosing a violent death for the name of Christ. The love of Jesus is beyond all love.

Jesus knelt with the lonely, broken and crippled. He stood with the sinful, he protected the condemned. Jesus chose a place of shame and guilt by eating with the notorious and the infamous. Every time that Jesus associated with sinful men and women, the attention was on them, the honour was deferred to them. Jesus' love for us is beyond our understanding, beyond our ability to express in words.

So how does this love affect me? How does my behaviour change, how does my church life change, my marriage, my friendships? Everything changes. Can I imagine a life where I genuinely put anyone before myself? Not really, it feels too far from the truth as it is today.

I heard a story recently about a world famous preacher. He was invited to talk to a Christian group in England. As the time grew closer the demand to hear him speak grew and grew. Soon the venue had changed four times, the capacity doubling with each change. When the evening of his address came about there were thousands in the room waiting to hear the great man speak. People took their seats and waited to hear what he had to say. The man walked onto the platform and many people rose to their feet and cheered him in. Others soon joined in, carried by the heightened atmosphere. Once the crowd had settled, the man walked to the lectern. He lifted his bible, and read, "Jesus said, 'love one another.'"

With that he paused. People leaned forward, waiting for comment, waiting for the next word. The man looked at the crowd before him. After about a minute people began to murmur. Time passed. The people complained to their neighbours about the anti-climax of it all. Then he repeated the line, "Jesus said, 'love one another.'"

The room fell silent. Within a few minutes many people were weeping. Many were receiving prayer, and many more were apologising and asking forgiveness of others. The bare reality of the simple command of Jesus came with such force on that room that people were changed forever. Let us no longer take this as a given. Let us love with a radical, life-changing love. Let us love like he did. Let us love.

Success

I remember standing in a row with seven friends in the worship tent of a Christian festival. There was a guy on stage getting quite excited. His voice got higher and higher in its pitch and more and more painful on my ears. I remember him repeating over and over again, "God is releasing amazing gifts to people in this room. World-changing gifts! People here will become famous evangelists, preachers and worship leaders. Prophets that will speak to millions are being birthed in this room."

Then one by one I saw the others in the room drop to their knees and call out to God for a part in these gifts. I remember feeling some sort of pressure to do the same. So I did. Within minutes a group of people in matching red t-shirts worked their way along the row speaking to each of us in turn. You will be a prophet; you will be a great preacher, etc etc.

For those I was with and for me it turned out that our lives took very different paths from those that were spoken over us. To be honest, I think in some cases we went in completely different directions from those suggested by the red army of zealous prayer ministers.

Why is it that everyone who is called to lead worship is promised greatness in terms of numbers and hearers and international ministry? I have been to three conferences in the past few years and at each one I have heard someone be prophesied over to that end. "You will take the mantel from Matt Redman or Tim Hughes." Like God has made room for only one major worship leader and we vie for the position.

I stood by recently and watched someone weep with joy as they heard the great ministry that was ahead of them. Phrases like "God-fame" and "international influence" are spoken again and again.

It's because of this kind of thing Christian conferences are the places I dread the most in Christendom. There is a part of me that loves them, and I would never suggest we stop them, but there are things that happen at them that I would love to avoid and I regularly run away from on the very rare occasions I attend a conference.

Rocks

My attention is always caught by the dramatic. It's true in every part of my life. I watch documentaries that report on exciting new discoveries or moving past glories. I like movies that twist at the end and take me by surprise. I like music that lifts into a crescendo and leaves you breathless.

I am also drawn towards the controversial. I love the people who say the things that everyone else thinks, but are too afraid to mention. Rob Bell, Don Miller, Derek Webb, Rich Mullins and Keith Green are all great heroes of mine and each of them has said some pretty controversial things.

I guess this affection for controversy is what draws me to Jesus. I love the stories where he refuses to wash his hands in the ceremonial way required by the other religious teachers. I love the way his friends were the wrong kind of people, the same people to whom today I'll be polite in church but from whom I will never get an invite for dinner.

The story about Jesus I love the most is so controversial, it is even debated as to whether it should be in the bible. The story of the adulteress in John 8 sends shivers through me every time I read it. It is dramatic and Jesus' words and actions fly in the face of every systematic theology I have ever formed about forgiveness.

Jesus is walking from the temple where he had been praying. Out of nowhere appears a crowd of the religious elite, the men who had been one step ahead of the rest their whole lives. They had always been the best of the best. They had good houses and demanded the respect of the people. They hated Jesus. He stood against their rules, he called them hypocrites: religious fraudsters who bound the weak with the chains of legalism.

The men had brought with them a sinful woman, an adulteress caught red handed. They threw her at Jesus' feet and read the list of her sins for all in the court to hear. They passed the judgement they felt she deserved and condemned her to death by stoning.

With stones in their hands the men's eyes moved from the broken spirit lying in the dirt and in her shame to Jesus. "In the Law Moses commanded us to stone such women. Now what do you say?" they asked him.

Jesus stepped forward in silence and stood between the woman and her accusers. He knelt down and wrote in the dirt. What he was writing has never been recorded and many have speculated. Another speculation will do no harm.

Jesus said that those who even look at a woman lustfully are guilty of adultery with her. I am sure these men knew his words well; they may have even heard his Sermon on the Mount.

I think Jesus wrote the names of the women these men had lusted for, the relationships they had sought on the side. He drew their minds back to his words. "If any one of you is without sin, let him be the first to throw a stone at her." With each name he wrote, another man made his excuses and left. Each one of them moved on, dropping his rocks as he went. In a short time there was only Jesus and the woman left.

"Woman, where are they? Has no one condemned you?" Jesus asked her. In my mind she looked up for the first time since she was thrown to the floor. She saw them gone and realised that she had been left alone with the only one who was sinless, the only one who could cast the first rock.

"...neither do I condemn you," Jesus declared. "Go now and leave your life of sin."

This story ruins my theology. I believe in forgiveness after repentance. Turn from your sin and be saved. This story flies in the face of that. Jesus offered forgiveness and then urged the woman to sin no more. He accepted her as an adulteress. For Jesus, a first century Jew, she was meant to be held in contempt, outcast, despised; but Jesus let her off the hook and she departed.

I am not like Jesus and I don't know many Christians who are. How many times have I looked in disgust at people whose sins are different from mine and demanded in my heart that they repent? How many times have I seen a person as a sin rather than as a person? I walked past a homeless drug addict today and refused him the pocket full of change that I was carrying. I chose to see a sin, not someone hungry and caught in a cycle of destruction he can't find a way out of.

I was reading John 8 a few days ago. I had just been reading an article in the Times newspaper about university Christian Unions being banned for their "homophobic" beliefs. I don't know how it happened but somehow evangelical beliefs regarding homosexuality dominate discussion on religion. The world snarls at the "homophobic" church and we growl back with equal force. We come up with clever quips about Adam and Steve. We write documents on our stance and the stance of our church, and the longer it goes on the deeper the trench that separates us becomes.

As I read the story the thought came to mind: what if these religious men had thrown a homosexual or a lesbian at the feet of Jesus?

Jesus knew the law; he knew adultery was against God's ideal in the same way he knew homosexuality was against God's ideal. The establishment stood with rocks in their hands and the law in their mouths. Jesus knelt on the ground with the law on his heart and forgiveness in his hands. When we look at the gay community who, according to our book, are choosing something we call sin, what are we holding? What are we saying? What are we thinking? Do we love them? Up to this point, I don't think I have done.

What if it had been me who they threw on the ground? What if it had been you? What does it take for Jesus to condemn you? At what point does Jesus say, "No, you're too far gone. Your sin is too uncomfortable for me, I can't forgive that." We do that very thing every day.

I choose selfishness and make conscious decisions to ignore the poor. I choose to buy a new coat over a coffee for a homeless man. I choose sin all the time. I don't slip and fall into sin; I choose it, and yet I am welcomed to speak and teach the bible. Every person who wears the Christian badge and claims to follow Jesus does the very same. They choose disobedience and blame the devil, but it is our fault. We choose sin every day. We are forgiven and loved by the church, yet so many people aren't because their sins are harder to hide than ours are.

I am writing this with a tension in my mind. I am uncomfortable with what it means that Jesus can just forgive someone with no guarantee of future purity. It scares me that this kind of teaching will fill our churches with people who don't fit the nice-middle-class-straight family picture that I choose to expect from church. It will draw in people who are choosing lives that I believe are against God's ideal. People who will fall in love with Jesus and still live lives of sin. People who will be forgiven and saved by grace but live in messed up relationships that rail against our beliefs. People who look a lot like me. Maybe that's what I'm afraid of.

Crutch

I read an article recently in which a Christian celebrity spoke of his clever response to those who claimed his Christianity was a crutch to get him through life. He made a few statements about manly, testosterone-fuelled spirituality and concluded that being a Christian was a sign of strength in a person rather than a crutch.

Growing up I heard this debate many times. In school as a 15-year-old Napoleon Dynamite look-alike I faced it all the time. It was a common view: people are Christians because they are weak. I remember trying to convince people I was strong, that I could do life well and be manly and aggressive just like everyone else.

In some ways I think that Jesus tackled a similar attitude towards faith in the religion of the Pharisees. These highly educated men had constructed for themselves a means by which they could do life; they could keep their own heads above water when the others drown. They read the law, the requirements they must meet in their lives as Jews and created rules for the law and rules for the rules for the law. They devoted their lives to keeping their rules, to keeping themselves right. They filled their lives with routine. They were strong men; they had control and discipline and the ability to get it right. Everyone else was sinking.

The Pharisees and the other rabbis (religious teachers) had a monopoly on God. They had the education, the wealth and the power. They owned religion. If any one wanted to encounter God they came through the rabbis. To meet God you had to behave, you had to meet the requirements that the rabbis set. You had to wash properly, eat properly, and work properly. You couldn't touch certain things; you couldn't go certain places or wear certain clothes. The longer the rabbis held control, the harder it became for the rest of us to make the grade.

How could a fisherman be ceremonially clean and make a living? How could a farmer? Or a midwife? They couldn't; they failed to be pure by the standards of their religious masters and gradually God became for the elite, for those who could bear the yoke of the rabbis and still eat.

When Jesus first stepped into the pulpit in the synagogue in Nazareth and read from the scroll of the Book of Isaiah, he set himself up as a rabbi. He was making a public declaration that he was joining the masters; he was part of the monopoly on God. He was opposed from day one. He didn't fit, he was a carpenter's son and he worked with his hands. It was the beginning of the strained relationship that he would have with the rabbis. It would only get worse.

On numerous occasions the other rabbis would challenge Jesus on his behaviour or the behaviour of his disciples. They ate corn on the Sabbath. He healed on the Sabbath. He didn't wash his hands properly. At a wedding he turned holy water, set aside for ceremonial washing, into wine. Over and over again Jesus seemed to be living in direct conflict with the rules of the rabbis but the people loved him.

One day Jesus finally admitted it. He summed up the rabbis' worries and clarified his position. "Follow me; the life you get carries a much lighter burden than the burden of the rabbis. My yoke is easy; my burden is light. Come with me, I am gentle, you will find rest for your souls."
(Well, that's my own paraphrase of what he said.)

Jesus' words resonated throughout the people. It spoke freedom to the farmer who felt rejected by God because he was constantly unclean. It spoke freedom to the lepers, the whores, and the drunks. None of them had access to God; they lived lives labelled as those who were untouchable, those who could never fulfil the requirements of the law. But here was a glimmer of hope, rest for their souls.

I read an article recently on one of those anonymous websites put together either by some young zealous theology student or a middle-aged man who never took the risk on ordination. If you search online for any popular preacher or writer of our times you'll find the sites I mean. These guys spend their free time writing articles exposing the lies and deception of the antichrists of mainstream thinking. The article was entitled something like "The Evangelical Sell Out – Tell Them What They Want To Hear". The writer wrote of his disgust at the modern church in its embracing of those whose teaching has gathered huge crowds. I remember one line that said something like, "as long as these Judases continue to replace the hard work of the gospel with the weak message of acceptance and love, their churches will continue to fill with self-seeking consumers."

It is almost like the brand of Christianity proposed on these sites is the modern version of a self-flagellating monastic lifestyle. This kind of thinking often goes hand in hand with long lists of rules and long lists of those who aren't real Christians. I'm happy to be proved wrong, but where is the love, joy, peace, patience, kindness, goodness, faithfulness and self control in a brand of faith that publicly calls its brother an anathema? I've had that label pinned on me by just such a brother and it hurts.

Unfortunately for some people this is the brand of Christian that they encounter first. The face of Christ they see is not the tear-filled, brokenhearted healer. It's the anger-fuelled, placard-waving proselytiser condemning anyone who steps one foot out of line.

Jesus' yoke is still easy, his burden is still light, and I need it to be. These days I am coming to terms with the idea that my faith is after all a crutch. The more I experience of faith, the more I realise that I can't do life. I am broken, I make bad decisions and let people down, and people let me down, and it hurts. Everyone one of us is this way and every one of us is scared to admit it. Life on earth is hard and we aren't very good at it. The more difficulties I face, the less I feel able to get through them, and as time runs on I become more and more aware of my limp. I can't walk through life, I have a limp, I stagger. Some days I can barely stand up under the weight of just existing in this broken place. If I am going to make it through I need a crutch to take my weight, to give me balance, to keep me upright to give me a chance to heal.

My mind goes back to that *Footprints* poem about the man walking on the beach. I think the conclusion is that God carries the man through the hard times, and the other times the man walks alongside God. I know it's sacrilege but I'm not sure it's a helpful picture, well not for me anyway. In my life, on my beach there is only one set of footprints – they're Jesus' prints. He's always carrying me. His yoke is easy and his burden is light because he's carrying them and me. He's much more than a crutch; he's everything.

Epilogue

So what do I do with these thoughts? What do I hope you do after reading them? I guess in some ways I am unsure, I didn't mean to write a book in the first place, so I didn't come at this with much of a strategy. Take from this what you need, I guess.

On reflection though I do hope that I have moved on from these thoughts, that I have begun to find answers to the questions and have grounded some of my beliefs in the day-to-day of my life.

I hope that for some people reading this will lead to them sharing their thoughts, that they will share their stories, their friendships and their pain with those around them. I hope that people will begin to say out loud what they have been feeling inside for a long time. If we can be honest with each other we can all move forward together.

I hope you can find in my stories and thoughts some answers to your questions or at least some affirmation that it is okay to have those questions in the first place.

I hope for some people there will be liberation, a freeing from the captivity of fake corporate piety.

I hope you will feel free to worship God as you are, warts and all, and glory in his undying love for you as you are, doubts, weakness, sin and humanity included.

I hope you will pursue a lifestyle of repentance, a constant acceptance of your position in the face of God's awesome holiness, that you would carve out a daily response to his grace and mercy.

I hope that you will learn to see beyond the symptoms of broken humanity and love those who are hidden behind their labels wanting to be accepted by the rest of us.

More than anything I hope you will find Jesus, that you will hear his voice calling to you from both the mundane and the glamorous. I hope that you will find in him all that you need, the answers to all your questions. I hope you will find him at the cross and allow the awesome power of that horrendous event to permeate your being and transform your heart.

If you're ever in York, let's have a coffee. I'd love to hear the stories of Jesus in your life.